THE
CATHEDRAL
AT WAWEL

I dedicate
this album to my Parents,
who first showed me the Cathedral

Stanisław Markowski

Graphic design
Lech Przybylski

Technical editor
Krystyna Brablec

ISBN 83-85833-02-1

THE
CATHEDRAL
AT WAWEL

Stanisław Markowski

AFTERWORD

Franciszek Ziejka

Translated by
William Brand

Post Scriptum
KRAKÓW

JEDNOŚĆ
KIELCE

...Everything here is Poland, every stone and every fragment,
and whoever enters here becomes a part of Poland, a part of this edifice.
We too now add to the measure of this body —
and, once we have entered inside these walls, we are Poland. (...)
Here, you can weep — and not one of your tears will be forgotten.
Rejoice — and none of your joy will be solitary.
Poland, eternally immortal, surrounds you.
Open your eyes ... — look, look, look,
and let the silence of your lips be the golden armour of your soul.

Stanisław Wyspiański 'Wyzwolenie' ('Liberation')

← Birds eye view of Cracow and Wawel

Dome of the Zygmunt Tower (19th–20th century,
Sławomir Odrzywolski)

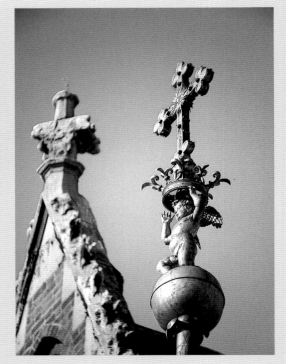

Fragments of copings and roofs

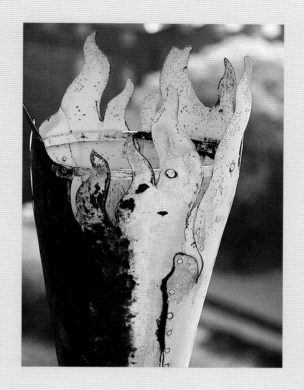

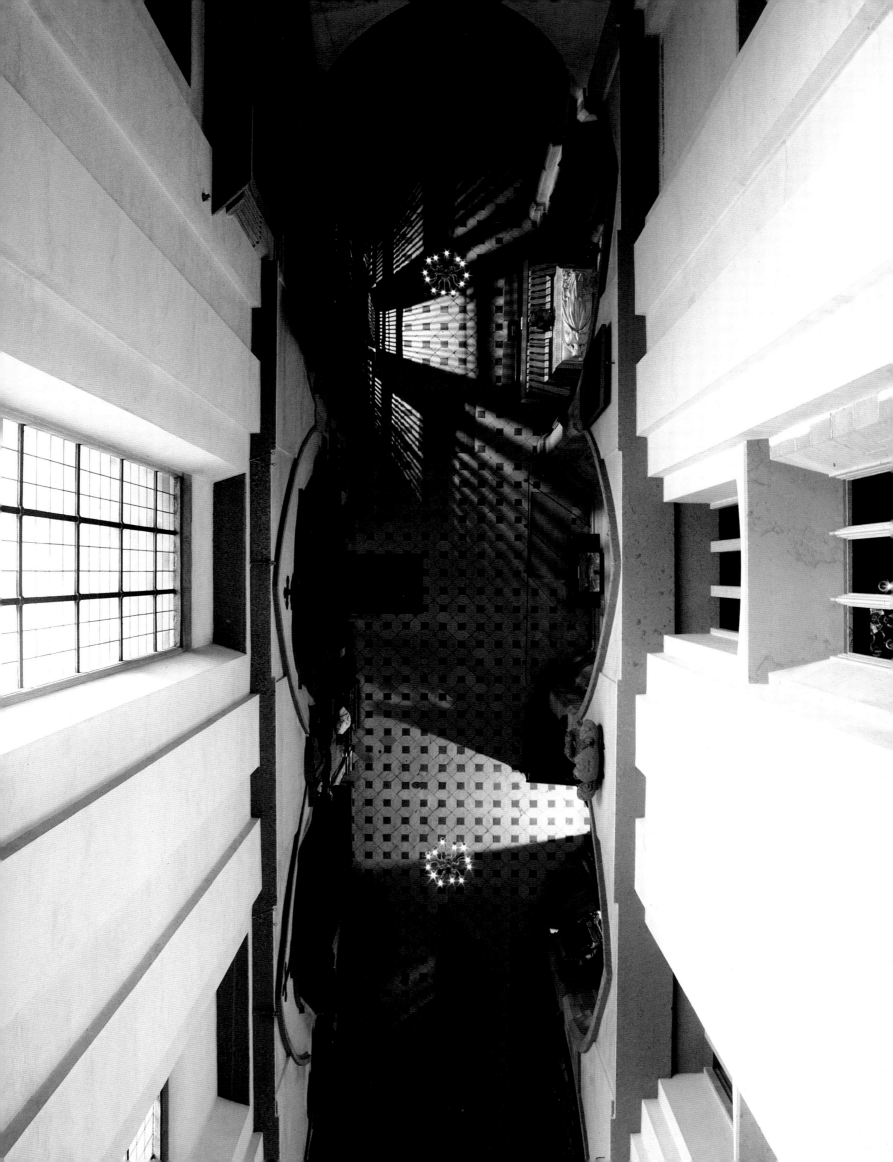

View onto the passage through the opening in the vaulting
← Passage (first half of the 14th century, rebuilt 1713–1715, Kacper Bażanka)

Passage. View of the vaulting

25   Presbytery (first half of the 14th century). View of the vaulting →

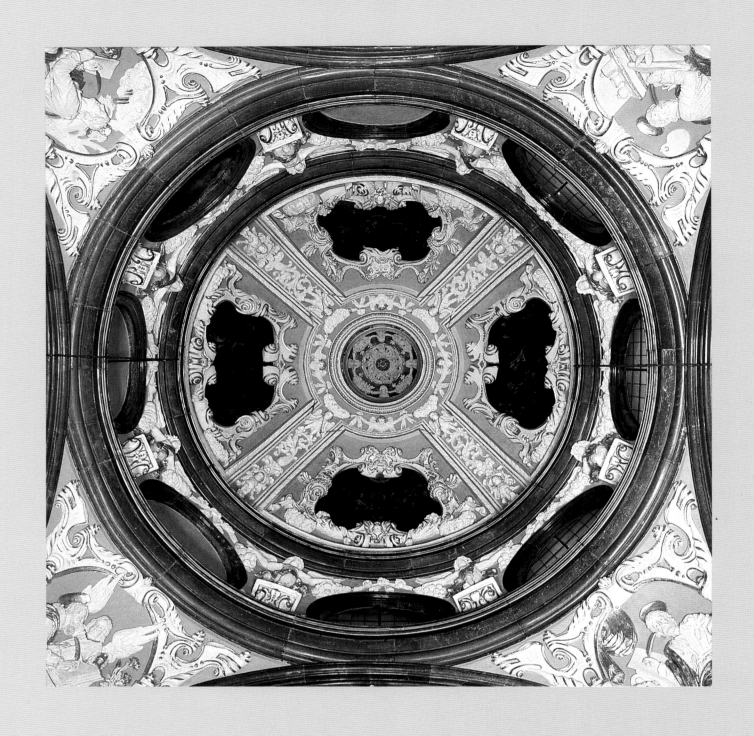

← Main nave (ca. mid-14th century). View of the vaulting

Cupola of the Waza Chapel (1664–1676)

29   Cupola of the Chapel of Bishop Jakub Zadzik (1645–1650)

Presbytery. View of the main altar
(mid-17th century, Giovanni Battista Gisleni)

43   Picture of the Crucifixion on the main altar (mid-17th century, Tommaso Dolabella [?],
Marcin Blechowski [?])

Passage

Passage →

Passage. View of the altar of the Miraculous Cross of Wawel.
At left, the tombs of King Jan III Sobieski and King Michał Korybut Wiśniowiecki

Fragments of the Miraculous Cross of Wawel (ca. 14th century) →

Fragments of arrases in the Presbytery (17th century)

Presbytery → 48

Fragment of arras from the main nave

Tiling in the main nave

Arrases from the main nave   62

Main nave. View of the choir →

65   View of the Confession of St. Stanisław from the choir

South nave →

Main entrance to the Cathedral →

Lipski Chapel. Tomb, fragment

Passage. Tomb, fragment

Arcade between the main and south naves.
Tombs of Piotr Kmita (late 16th century) and Andrzej Ciekliński (late 16th century)

Passage. Memorial stone of Stanisław Borek (1558)

Passage. Epitaph portraits of Jan Tarło, Stanisław Chomentowski, and Krzysztof Szembek (late 18th century)

Lipski Chapel. Fragment of the monument to Bishop Andrzej Lipski (ca. 1634)

Presbytery. Tombstone of Cardinal Fryderyk Jagiellończyk
(1510, studio of Peter Vischer, Nuremburg)

South nave. Piotr Boratyński memorial (1559)

Passage. Fragments of memorials

73   Holy Cross Chapel (third quarter of the 15th century). Interior view

Holy Cross Chapel. Painting from an interior panel of the Holy Trinity triptych (1467).
Chorus of prophets

Holy Cross Chapel. Painting from an interior panel of the Holy Trinity triptych.
Chorus of virgins

Holly Cross Chapel. Paintings from an exterior panel of the Holy Trinity triptych:

The Conversion of Paul

The Vision of St. Eustace

St. George slaying the dragon

The travails of Secundus

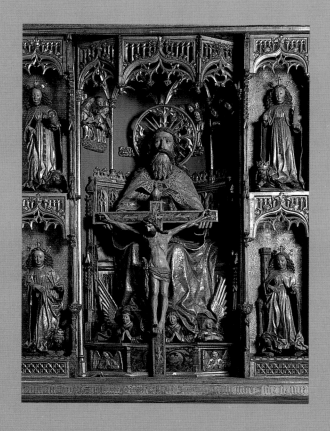

75

Holy Cross Chapel. Central section of the Holy Trinity triptych.
Fragments

Holy Cross Chapel. Frescoed vaulting (1470, Pskov school)
and Polish eagle (third quarter of the 15th century). Fragments

Holy Cross Chapel. Kibitka on the memorial of Bishop Kajetan Sołtyk (1789)

Zygmunt Chapel. Silver Altar (1531–1538, bas-relief by Melchior Baier
89   after Peter Flötner, painting by Jerzy Pencz)

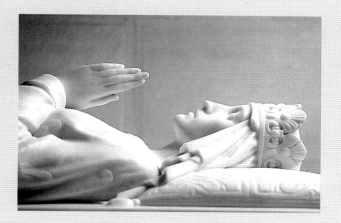

← Memorial of Queen Jadwiga (1902, Antoni Madeyski)

Memorial of Queen Jadwiga. Fragments

Funereal inscription of Queen Jadwiga

93   Memorial of King Kazimierz the Great (Wielki; after 1370)

Memorial of King Kazimierz the Great. Canopy

Memorial of King Kazimierz the Great. Fragment

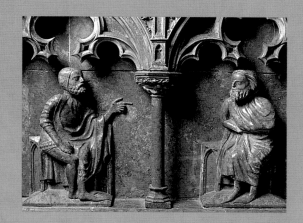

Memorial of King Kazimierz the Great. Fragments

King Jan Olbracht Chapel. Memorial of the king (1502–1505; niche, Francesco the Florentine; statue, Jörg Huber [?])

97   Bishop Filip Padniewski memorial (ca. 1575, Jan Michałowicz of Urzędów)

Skotnicki Chapel. Memorial of Michał Skotnicki (1809, Stefano Ricci)

Entry to the Treasury →

← Interior of the Treasury
(late 15th century, rebuilt,
painting on vault, early 20th century, Józef Mehoffer)

Spear of St. Maurice —
offered in 1000 to Bolesław the Brave (Chrobry) by Otto III

Monstrance (17th century)

Gothic chalice (16th century)

112

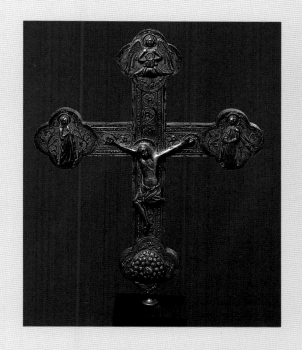

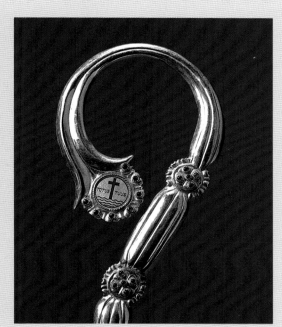

Romanesque processional cross (13th century)

Cross (1472–1488)
with fragments of the 13th century crowns
of Bolesław the Bashful (Wstydliwy) and Kinga

Silver crozier (17th century)

Crozier of Archbishop Karol Wojtyła (Pope John Paul II)

Eigitur clementissime
pater per ihm xpm filui
tuu dominu nrm supplices
rogamus ac petimus :
vti accepta habeas ⁊ be
nedicas hec do ✠ na hec mu ✠ nera
hec san ✠ cta sacrificia illibata In pri
mus que tibi offerimus pro ecclesia tua
sancta catholica · quam pacificare custodire

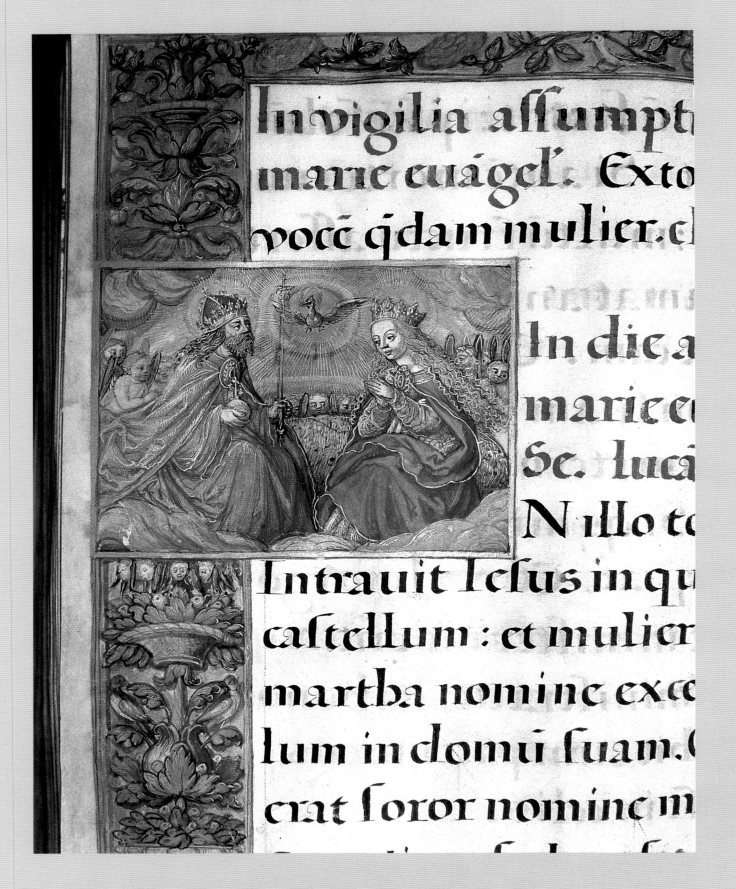

In vigilia assumpt

marie euágel'. Exto

vocē q dam mulier. d

In die a

marice

Se. luci

N illo te

Intrauit Iesus in qu

castellum : et mulier

martha nomine exce

lum in domū suam.

erat soror nomine m

'Missale' (1440). The Martyrdom of St. Stanisław

127 ← Entrance to the crypt of the poets Adam Mickiewicz and Juliusz Słowacki

Crypt of Adam Mickiewicz and Juliusz Słowacki

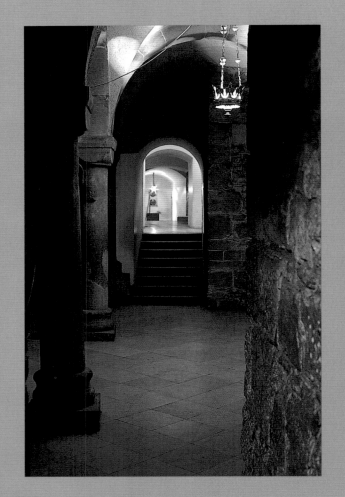

Entrance to the crypt of St. Leonard

Crypt of St. Leonard (11th–12th centuries) →

Crypt of Marshal Józef Piłsudski (1930's)

Waza and Zygmunt Chapels

View from the southwest →

← Tower of the Silver Bells

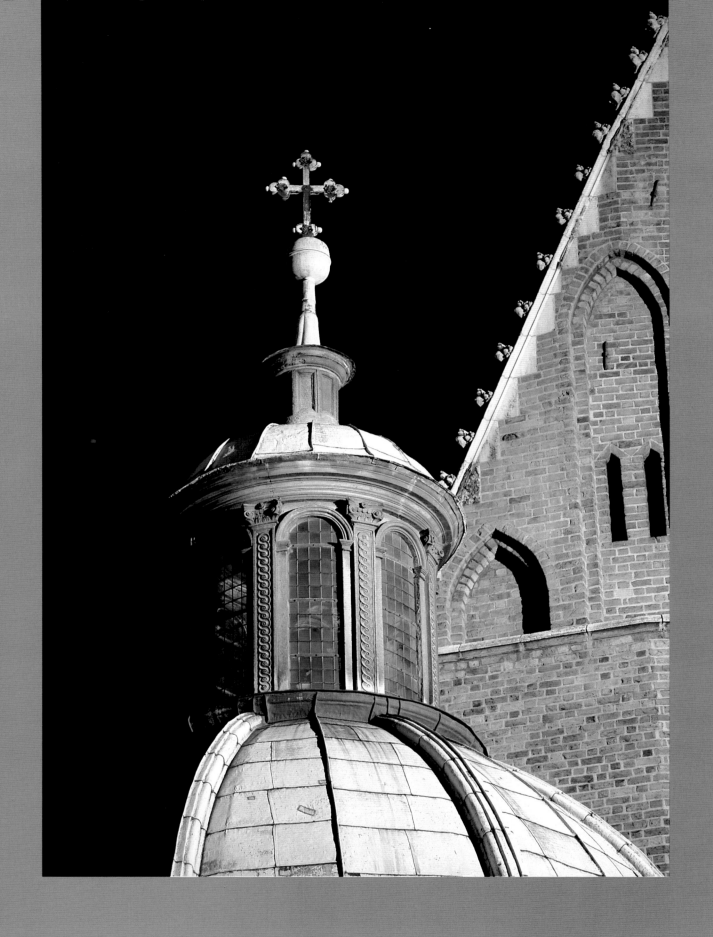

Lantern of the cupola of the Waza Chapel

Cupolas of the Waza and Zygmunt Chapels. Transept →

154

Tower of the Silver Bells. Fragment

Barrel of the Zygmunt Chapel. Fragment →

Western gates of the Cathedral cemetery. Fragment

Before the Cathedral house

View from the west

Peak of the facade
(mid-14th century)

Statue of St. Stanislaw
(copy of 14th-century sculpture)
on the peak of the facade

161

Portal of the main entrance (1636–1639)
and doors donated by King Kazimierz the Great, with his monogram →

View of Wawel from the northwest

The Vistula and Wawel

THE POLISH SHRINE
AT WAWEL

Franciszek Ziejka

and flee the country. Bishop Stanislaus' cult grew until he was canonized.
It is also worth mentioning Bishop Wincenty Kadłubek. He was one of the first
Poles to study at the Sorbonne in Paris. Upon returning home, he worked
in the chancery of Prince Casimir the Just (Kazimierz Sprawiedliwy). In
1208 he was elected Bishop of Cracow, and in 1215 he took part in the Lateran
Council. Three years later, he made a stunning decision: he left Wawel and
journeyed on foot from the Cathedral to the Cistercian monastery in
Jędrzejów, where he entered the novitiate and became a monk. Later, he
would write his 'Chronicle of Poland' there. He was beatified in 1764.

Another outstanding figure was Bishop Jan Prandota. He ascended to the
bishopric in 1242. For many years, he was one of the closest associates of
Prince Bolesław the Bashful (Wstydliwy). He owes his place in the history
of the Cracow Church to his leading role in the canonization of St. Stanislaus.
Upon his death in 1266, Bishop Prandota was interred in the former chapel of
SS. Peter and Paul. The accidental discovery of his tomb in the mid-fifteenth
century revived the memory of his services. For a time, preparations were
even made to push for his canonization, but the intention was later forgotten.
During the reconstruction of the chapel of SS. Peter and Paul in 1639, the
remains of this revered bishop were transferred to the wall of the chapel.

The foremost statesman among all the earlier bishops of Cracow was
doubtless Zbigniew Oleśnicki. He had already made a lasting name for himself
at the Battle of Grunwald, when he was only 21. Długosz describes in detail
his knightly valour. Oleśnicki was among the personal retinue of King
Władysław Jagiełło. When the Knight of Meissen, Dypold von Kökritz, broke
through in a surprise attack on the Polish king, Oleśnicki managed to intervene
at the very last moment and knock von Kökritz from his mount. In 1423,
Oleśnicki received the bishopric of Cracow. His exceptional intellect soon
made him the most influential politician of his time. He played an especially
important role during the reign of Władysław III, later known as Warneńczyk,
and in the first years of the reign of the latter's brother, Casimir the Jagiellon.
As bishop of Cracow he cared for the diocese, fostering the cults of St. Stanislaus
and of the Apostles to the Slavs, SS. Cyril and Methodius. He also
campaigned for the canonization of Queen Jadwiga. He introduced the
Corpus Christi procession to Cracow. He also left his mark on scholarship:
on his initiative, Jan Długosz wrote his multi-volume work on the history of Poland,
'Twelve Books of Polish History'. A provision of Oleśnicki's will was the founding
of the 'Jerusalem Bursary' (on the site of the present-day Collegium Novum)
for students of the Cracow Academy, to which he also donated his library.

The history of the bishopric of Cracow in the sixteenth century is above all the
story of patronage of the arts and culture. First came Bishop Piotr Tomicki, an
outstanding humanist, diplomat and politician, a bibliophile and the creator of
a splendid library. It was Tomicki who hired Bartolomeo Berrecci to rebuild the
Chapel of St. Thomas. In 1533, Bishop Tomicki consecrated the Sigismund Chapel.

Nor can we pass over Bishop Samuel Maciejowski, who ascended to the
throne of St. Stanislaus in 1546. A close associate and even a friend of King
Sigismund Augustus (Zygmunt August), he will always be remembered in

the Cracow Church as a shrewd politician, a pastor who tended the development of the Church, and a defender of the bonds of matrimony (at the Piotrków Assembly in 1548, he hotly defended the validity of Sigismund Augustus's marriage with Barbara Radziwiłłówna). As Chancellor of the University, he fought to hold the standards of scholarship at a high level. In Wawel Cathedral, Bishop Maciejowski rebuilt the Chapel of Our Lady of the Snows in Renaissance style and endowed a gorgeous high altar.

Several other Cracow bishops of the Golden Age, each of whom left his own mark on Polish culture, deserve our attention. Bishop Piotr Myszkowski, whose lovely memorial adorns the Różyc Chapel that he restored in Wawel Cathedral, was the friend and protector of such writers as Jan Kochanowski and Klemens Janicki. Bishop Filip Padniewski was an eminent humanist, orator, and historian.

Among later shepherds of the Cracow flock, Bishop Marcin Szyszkowski, who ran the diocese for fifteen years at the beginning of the seventeenth century, deserves mention first. He came to power when the King and Court had left Cracow for good, and this gave him additional responsibilities, not only to the Cathedral but to the whole city. It was Szyszkowski who employed Giovanni Battista Trevano in 1626–1631 to erect the Confession of St. Stanislaus, which takes the breath away even today: this is the free-standing canopied altar in the centre of the Cathedral, covered by a golden cupola. Bishop Szyszkowski also founded the Cathedral Choir and the College of Angelists. Nor can we forget Bishop Piotr Gembicki, whose greatest service was to the Polish state as Great Crown Chancellor, but who served the Church as bishop in 1642–1657. He financed the general renovation of the Cathedral Treasury and the new High Altar that still ornaments Wawel Cathedral today, covered the roof with copper, and ordered the new coffin for the relics of St. Stanislaus.

As long as we are summoning up individuals from among the bishops of the Cracow diocese, we must spend some time on the tragic figure of Bishop Ignacy Kajetan Sołtyk, who ascended to the bishopric in 1759. He is known in national history as one of the first victims of persecution by Tsarina Catherine II. During an assembly of the 'sejm' or Polish parliament in Warsaw, he and four other senators were abducted on the night of October 13, 1767, and exiled to Kaluga in Siberia on the orders of the Russian ambassador in Warsaw, Nikolai V. Repnin. Sołtyk spent five years in exile and returned suffering from an incurable disease from which he died in 1788. A year later, Michał Sołtyk funded a tomb for the bishop-exile in Holy Cross Chapel, on which is depicted the scene of the deceased's transportation to Kaluga.

The era of the Polish partitions left its scars on the history of the Cracow episcopacy. In 1830, Father Karol Wincenty Skórkowski became bishop. He supported the unsuccessful November Uprising and, in reprisal, the Russian authorities forbade him the exercise of episcopal authority in the parts of the Cracow diocese that lay in the Kingdom of Poland, which was under Russian control. Then the Austrian authorities banned him from pastoral work in Cracow, so he had no choice but to go into exile in Opawa in Silesia, where he died in 1851.

When his remains were returned to Cracow so that he could be buried in the Cathedral in accordance with tradition, the Austrian authorities turned the funeral cortege away from the gates of the city.

As a result of this oppression, the diocese of Cracow was left without a bishop for 44 years. It was managed by administrators. Only in 1879 did the Austrian authorities relent and approve the restitution of the office of bishop. The Pope called Father Albin Dunajewski to the throne of St. Stanislaus. Dunajewski had a splendid biography: in his youth, he had been a member of the secret Society of the Polish People, for which in 1841 an Austrian court sentenced him to death. On appeal, the sentence was commuted eight years imprisonment in the Spielberg fortress in Brno. During the January Uprising of 1863, Dunajewski openly supported the rebels, as a result of which he had to leave Warsaw. In the history of the Cracow Diocese, he is remembered for his decision to undertake the general restoration of the Cathedral at the last minute, before the edifice fell into ruin.

Nor could we, finally, pass over in silence the figure of Cardinal Adam Stefan Sapieha, who ruled Wawel Cathedral for forty years (1912–1951). He initiated the office of Diocesan Conservator and the Artistic Advisory Committee for the Restoration of Wawel Cathedral. Bishop Sapieha rescued the royal coffins from destruction when they were suddenly attacked by an unfamiliar form of tin corrosion in the 1920's. He financed the restoration of the Cathedral's collection of gobelin arrases and liturgical paraments, as well as the miraculous cross of Queen Jadwiga and the crypt of St. Leonard. The list of Cardinal Sapieha's services to the Cathedral could be made much, much longer.

The tenure in office as bishop of Cracow of Karol Wojtyła, who undertook the rebuilding of the Cracow Church and the Polish Church, must be regarded as a Golden Age. An important stage in this great undertaking was the celebration of the Millennium of Polish Christianity and the accompanying procession of the Painting of the Blessed Virgin of Częstochowa (the 'Black Madonna') around the archdiocese. Between 1972 and 1979, during the nine hundredth anniversary of Stanislaus of Szczepanów's tenure as bishop, he led the great Cracow Synod, aimed at fully bringing the teachings of the Second Vatican Council to life. The ceremonial sessions were held in Wawel Cathedral. As Pope John Paul II, Cardinal Wojtyła has continued on a worldwide scale the work that he began in Cracow. After his election to the See of Peter, he was succeeded as protector of Wawel Cathedral and the whole Archdiocese by Cardinal Franciszek Macharski. He was at the helm in Wawel Cathedral in the declining days of communism, when that system tried to defend itself against the people through the introduction of martial law and the persecution of the opposition. Wawel Cathedral became a centre of support for 'Solidarity'. Solemn Masses for the Fatherland were celebrated, and patriotic demonstrations set out from the Cathedral on national anniversaries.

CORONATION
SHRINE

Historians tend to regard Cracow as the capital of the state from the time of Casimir the Renewer. Casimir's two sons, Bolesław the Bold and Władysław Herman, went on to reside here. Cracow was also designated the senior region of Poland in the testament of Władysław's son, Bolesław the Wry-Mouthed, which divided the country among the latter's sons in 1138. The canonization of St. Stanislaus in the mid-thirteenth century settled things once and for all: whoever controlled Cracow had the right to regard himself as ruler of all the Polish lands. It is therefore not at all strange that when Władysław Łokietek finally reunited the regions of the country and began working towards his own coronation, he had no intention of returning to Gniezno, where the first kings of Poland had been crowned. He designated Wawel as the cathedral in which he would be crowned.

This first coronation in Cracow took place on January 20, 1320, when the old shrine erected by Herman was still in use. Jan Długosz has left an extensive description. Several bishops, many abbots, priests, and 'a great crowd of gentlemen' took part. On the day before the ceremony, Władysław Łokietek made a pilgrimage on foot from Wawel to Skałka (the Church 'on the Rock'), where Bishop Stanislaus had been murdered. This custom became an obligation of Polish kings from the times of Władysław Jagiełło's son, Władysław Warneńczyk, on. It cannot be ruled out that Casimir the Great, and perhaps even Jagiełło, had made the pilgrimage to Skałka. Even Henryk Walezy (Henry of Valois), who knew little enough about the history of Poland, followed this custom. So did the last king of Poland, Stanisław August Poniatowski, who despite having been crowned in Warsaw took part in a procession from Wawel to Skałka during his one and only visit to the former Polish capital, in 1787.

The second coronation in Wawel Cathedral, of Łokietek's son, Casimir the Great, evoked a great deal of confusion. Łokietek probably died on March 2, 1333. His successor immediately began preparing for his own coronation. The Queen Mother, Jadwiga, then unexpectedly entered onto the scene, issuing

a statement that so long as she was alive, she would not assent to the coronation
of a new queen — Casimir's wife, Anna. Only the repeated urging of her
son broke down the Queen Mother's opposition. On April 25, 1333,
Archbishop Janisław of Gniezno (the same one who had crowned Łokietek)
placed the crowns on the heads of Casimir and Anna in Wawel Cathedral.
The Queen Mother removed herself for the occasion to the convent of
the Poor Clares in Stary Sącz.

An extraordinary coronation took place in Wawel Cathedral on October 16,
1384. This time it was a girl of ten (or, as some historians have it, 14),
the Hungarian Princess Jadwiga, great-niece of Casimir the Great, who was
crowned Queen of Poland. From the moment of her coronation Jadwiga
was given the authority to rule Poland 'until they search out a suitable spouse
for her', as the chronicler noted. It took two years of searching to locate a candidate
for husband of the queen: he was Jagiełło, Duke of Lithuania, who came
to Cracow with his brothers at the beginning of 1386. A historic ceremony
took place in Wawel Cathedral on February 15, 1386: Archbishop Bodzanta
baptized Jagiełło and three of his brothers. Three days later, Jagiełło married
Queen Jadwiga, and on March 4 he was crowned King of Poland.

Guests came to Cracow from all over Europe on March 5, 1424, for the
coronation of Jagiełło's fourth wife, Zofia Holszańska — the 'Sonka' who was
famous for her beauty and largesse. They included Emperor Sigismund of
Luxembourg, King Eric of Denmark, and dozens of princes and bishops. The
legendary last Crusader of Europe, Władysław Warneńczyk, had two coronations
in Wawel Cathedral. First, when he was ten years old in 1434, he was crowned King
of Poland. Six years later, on March 8, 1440, the Hungarian crown was
placed upon his head. Three years passed between his tragic death in the Battle
of Varna in 1444 and the coronation of his successor. This was because his
body was never found on the battlefield, and he could therefore not be proved
dead. Finally, however, his brother Casimir was crowned at Wawel on
June 25, 1447.

There is no need to describe all the subsequent coronations at Wawel. On the other hand, it would be a shame not to mention the wedding of King Sigismund I to the Italian princess Bona Sforza. The King's darling arrived from the principality of Bari on April 15, 1518 in the company of more than a thousand knights and lords (a scrupulous chronicler enumerated 790 horses in her escort!). The combined royal wedding and coronation of Queen Bona took place on April 18, 1518. 'At ten o'clock', as a historian writes, 'the coronation procession set out from the castle along a road laid with a red carpet. The King entered in his crown and in a scarlet cloak lined with sable. Before him walked the Chancellor, Krzysztof Szydłowiecki, with the sceptre, and the voivode of Poznań, Mikołaj Lubrański, with the apple. Immediately behind Sigismund followed Bona in a splendid turquoise gown embroidered with gold. The ceremonies were watched by crowds of Cracovians gathered on Wawel Hill. Primate Jan Łaski concelebrated mass with the Bishop of Cracow, Jan Konarski and the Bishop of Poznań, Jan Lubrański. After the act of marriage, the Primate performed the coronation of Bona'.

In the mid-sixteenth century, there were dramatic political events connected with the efforts by Sigismund Augustus (the son of Sigismund I and Bona) to have the 'sejm' (parliament) acknowledge his marriage to Barbara Radziwiłłówna. Sigismund Augustus had been crowned at the age of ten, in 1530, while his father was still alive. After the death of his first wife, Elizabeth of Austria, Sigismund Augustus secretly married Barbara, daughter of the Chamberlain of Wilno, Jerzy Radziwiłł, in 1547. A year later, he ascended to the throne. Both the Queen Mother and the majority of senators and delegates to the 'sejm' refused to recognize the King's marriage with Barbara Radziwiłłówna. Sigismund Augustus battled long and hard for his wife's right to the royal crown. Finally, on February 13, 1549, Barbara made her ceremonial entrance to Wawel. She was greeted in the Cathedral with a beautiful speech, delivered in Polish, by Piotr Myszkowski, the future bishop of Cracow. A year later, on December 7, 1550, Barbara was crowned in Wawel Cathedral.

Also dramatic was the coronation of the first elected king, Henry of Valois. The ceremony took place on February 21, 1574. During the negotiations preceding the election of Henry, it was established among other provisions that during his coronation the king would pledge peace with people of other faiths. Henry agreed to this condition. When the moment came, however, the canny Henry omitted the relevant passage from the vows he swore on the steps of the altar. The Marshal protested at the last moment, and threatened to remove the crown from the Cathedral. 'The King had to take his vows again, this time in a corrected version, and for a second time he received the crown from the hands of the Primate', stated an eyewitness.

An incident of great symbolic importance took place during the magnificent coronation ceremony of Władysław IV Vasa on February 6, 1633. Albrecht Radziwiłł, a participant in the events, writes that 'after the Elevation, the crown began to slide from the king's head, so he gave me the apple to hold and, adjusting the crown himself, said to me, "This crown is heavier than I thought, but it seems to me that its meaning is even heavier"'. So it was in fact. Many a storm awaited this king in his fifteen-year reign.

S. Michaelis

Coronation ceremonies were usually organized directly after the selection of a new king. Only John III Sobieski was an exception to this rule. He was elected king in 1674, but postponed his coronation in view of the continuing war against the Turks. He only came to Cracow at the end of January 1676, and — together with Maria Kazimiera — accepted the crown on February 2 of that year.

The last coronation in Wawel Cathedral took place on January 17, 1734. On that day, the Bishop of Cracow, Jan Aleksander Lipski, crowned Augustus III of Saxony and his wife, as King and Queen of Poland. On the strength of a law passed by the 'sejm' in May, 1764, King Stanisław August was crowned in St. John's Church in Warsaw. Unfortunately, the law did not elaborate upon the 'important reasons' for taking the decision.

Along with the fall of the Polish state, matters connected with the crowning of the Polish Kings fell into oblivion. The regalia used in the coronation ceremonies was also lost. It was the Prussians who were responsible for this profanation. Shortly before they occupied Cracow in 1795, the Prussian king Frederick Wilhelm II issued an order that insignia of the Polish monarchy be confiscated. The Commandant of the City of Cracow and the Chief Chamberlain of the Prussian king immediately went into action. They spread word through the city that they were offering a large reward to anyone who would point out where the royal treasury was hidden on Wawel. They quickly found the traitor they were looking for: he was the very man who had been assigned to defend the treasures against the enemy. A locksmith brought in from Wrocław could not deal with the seven locks on the doors of the treasury, so a stone ram was used to break through the wall and provide access to the strongroom. On October 4, 1795, all the Polish regalia was carried off — by way of Wrocław — to the Prussian treasury. In 1809, it was melted down.

This is how historians present the account of the Polish regalia. Among Cracovians, however, a folk legend has persisted which tells a different story. According to this legend, the royal crowns were smuggled out of Wawel by Polish patriots at the last moment before the entry of the Prussians, and hidden in a safe place. The secret of their location is supposed to have been handed down from father to son, 'until the right time comes for revealing the secret'. Thus, although it lost its independence, the nation did not lose hope. This hope has been sustained above all by Wawel Cathedral, the guardian of national memories and the living wellspring of the rebirth of Poland. And the Cathedral has indeed always sheltered a great treasure: the tombs of kings and heroes. They have given successive generations of Poles hope in a better future.

POLISH
NECROPOLIS

The popular turn-of-the-century painter Wincenty Wodzinowski created a picture called 'All Saints' Day in Wawel Cathedral', which depicts a religious ceremony at the crypt of St. Leonard. The faithful who have gathered to pray are an unusual group: the kings of Poland, starting with Mieszko and Bolesław the Brave. The painting reflects the old custom of saying mass for the souls of the Polish kings and national heroes at the oldest crypt in the Wawel shrine on All Saints' Day. These prayers for the souls of the departed kings were one way of keeping the consciousness of the continuity of statehood alive in the mind of the nation. Even when no Polish state was to be found on the maps, it still existed in the hearts of the people — and it also existed here, on Wawel Hill. The tombs of the kings would become one of the foundation stones of the future independent state.

The earthly remains of at least several hundred people rest in the crypts of the Wawel Cathedral. They include several dozen bishops (most commonly in stone boxes, without coffins and also without inscriptions), fourteen kings, many queens, and dozens of royal offspring. There is also place for many high dignitaries, and also for national heroes and for the greatest poets. For nearly a thousand years this shrine has served as a cemetery. Beside the saints and the blessed, it holds the ashes of warriors and statesmen; beside great priests, eminent patrons of the arts; beside the aged, children. In the stone crypts of this church, Poles have placed the creators of their national history. There is a great host of them.

Unfortunately, we know little about the earliest burials in Wawel Cathedral. The chroniclers tell us, for instance, that Casimir the Renewer's wife Dobrogniewa was laid to rest here, and also Mieszko, the son of Bolesław the Bold. This is also the eternal resting place of Bolesław the Curly, (Kędzierzawy), Casimir the Just, Leszek the White (Biały) who was poisoned in Gąsawa. Many bishops were buried here in the first centuries of Polish history. Today, however, we seek in vain the graves of these rulers and churchmen. They were destroyed at the time of the construction of the present Gothic Cathedral. It is reasonable

to assume that only the tombs themselves were destroyed, and the remains of the deceased preserved. Where they were preserved, however, is difficult to say.

The oldest tombs to be found in the Cathedral are in the crypt of St. Leonard. The earliest royal tomb still preserved in the Cathedral is the sarcophagus of Władysław Łokietek, ornamented with a bas-relief of attractive simplicity and directness. Władysław Łokietek's son Casimir the Great had two funerals in Wawel Cathedral. The first, on November 19, 1370, was carried out through the efforts of his successor, Louis of Hungary. Casimir's second funeral took place five centuries after the first, in 1869. The sepulchral chamber of the great ruler had been uncovered during restoration work on the Cathedral. After its investigation by a commission, a ceremonial reinterment was held on July 8, 1869. The funeral procession wended its way from the Church of the Blessed Virgin on the Main Square to the Cathedral, but there was, of course, no contemporary ruler of Poland to lead it.

Only four monarchs have been honoured with burial in the naves of the Cathedral. The others are Jadwiga (who rests beside the high altar) and Władysław Jagiełło. The majority of the bishops, and kings (Casimir the Jagiellon, John Albert, and Stefan Batory) are buried in the chapels. Sigismund I the Old (Stary) initiated the tradition of interment in crypts built beneath chapels bearing the name of the monarch. From 1644 on, kings were also buried in crypts beneath the Vasa Chapel. The last royal funeral in Wawel Cathedral took place on January 15, 1734, when Augustus II of Saxony was laid to rest in the crypts.

After Poland lost its independence, national heroes began to be buried in Wawel Cathedral. The body of Prince Józef Poniatowski was entombed in the crypt of St. Leonard in 1817. A year later, the ostentatious funeral ceremony of Tadeusz Kościuszko took place. Both of these champions of freedom would eventually lie in beautiful sarcophagi: Ferdynand Kuhn sculpted a marble sarcophagus for Prince Józef in 1830, while Paweł Filippi executed Kościuszko's sarcophagus after Francesco Maria Lanci's design in 1832. In 1819, the Senate of the City of Cracow approved a resolution to lay the remains of a third great national hero, General Jan Henryk Dąbrowski, to rest in Wawel Cathedral. Unfortunately, the partitioning powers opposed this idea so strongly that it was never carried out. The man who had formed the Polish Legions in Italy during the Napoleonic Wars thus lies on the Winnogóra estate in Poznań province, which had been given to him as a reward for his military services. In Wawel, he is honoured only by a small plaque bearing the inscription: 'From the Representatives of the Nation to the Hero, Dąbrowski'.

Many years were spent in the effort to honour the memories of the great Polish Romantic poets by bringing their ashes from cemeteries in Paris to Wawel Cathedral. In the case of Adam Mickiewicz it took twenty-one years (from 1869 until 1890) and for Juliusz Słowacki it took thirty years (from 1897 until 1927). Marshal Józef Piłsudski was buried in Wawel Cathedral in 1935. Since 1937, the Marshal's coffin has lain in a crypt specially prepared for it beneath the Tower of the Silver Bells.

After the Second World War, when the guns had barely fallen silent, Cardinal Prince Adam Sapieha permitted the grave of Queen Jadwiga to be opened on July 12, 1949. He took part himself. Two days later, the remains of Queen Jadwiga were reinterred in the sarcophagus in the south nave of the Cathedral, during a modest ceremony. During his third pilgrimage to Poland, in 1987, Pope John Paul II performed the elevation of the relics of the Blessed Queen Jadwiga, which were placed in the altar of the Miraculous Cross.

In 1972, Cardinal Wojtyła permitted the opening of the graves of King Casimir the Jagiellon and his wife Elżbieta Rakuszanka, in the Holy Cross Chapel. After scientific research and preservation work were carried out, the royal pair were laid to rest again on October 18, 1973. Although a king of Poland was being buried, no representative of the secular authorities was present. However, members of the Polish Council of Bishops took part, along with Cardinal Wojtyła and the Primate, Cardinal Stefan Wyszyński.

ALTAR
OF THE FATHERLAND

From earliest times, the cathedral — the church of the bishops of Cracow — has functioned as a national shrine. The tomb of St. Stanislaus, who has been recognized since 1254 as the 'Patron of the Fatherland', has filled the role of 'Altar of the Fatherland' (Ara Patriae) since the fourteenth century. Here, prayers have been said for the blessing of wars in defence of the homeland. News has been brought here of the progress of these wars and the trophies of war have been deposited here: banners, ensigns, and standards. There is nothing strange about the fact that for the ancestors of today's Poles, Wawel Cathedral with its Altar of the Fatherland was a visible sign of the majesty of the Republic.

The tradition of depositing the trophies of victory in the shrine at Wawel began with Władysław Łokietek. In 1331, he brought to Wawel a banner won from the Teutonic Knights at the Battle of Płowce. Władysław Jagiełło continued this tradition after the Battle of Grunwald (1410). In 1411, a special ceremony was organized, during which the victor of the greatest battle of the Middle Ages placed on the altar of St. Stanislaus fifty-one banners captured from the Teutonic Knights. The tradition grew down the years. Not only kings, but also army commanders and even private persons carried their trophies to Wawel.

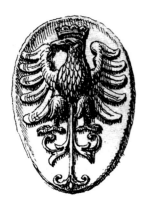

Ceremonies in solemn honour of great events in the life of the nation were organized in the Cracow Cathedral.

However, Wawel Cathedral was always more than a place of prayer. It offered succour to the country in times of need. In 1655, part of the silver collection of the Cathedral treasury was donated to the furnishing of the army being raised against the Swedish invasion. A large part of the Cathedral's treasure was turned over to Commander Tadeusz Kościuszko in 1794 when the latter called upon the nation to rise up and fight for its independence. Not surprisingly, kings endowed the shrine with the greatest respect. John Casimir arrived in Cracow the day after the Swedes left the city in 1657 to express

193

his thanksgiving to God in the Wawel sanctuary. John III Sobieski had special esteem for the Cathedral. Before setting out on the military expedition to Vienna that would save Europe from the Turkish threat, he prayed at the tomb of St. Stanislaus. On August 10, 1683, the papal nuncio granted a blessing to the king and the whole army during a pontifical high mass. After the victory, the king personally brought the greatest of the trophies he had won at Vienna, the grand banner of the Vizier, to the tomb of St. Stanislaus.

National heroes continued this monarchical tradition during the years when the nation had lost its independence. After his victory over the Russian army at the Battle of Racławice in 1794, Tadeusz Kościuszko hurried to Wawel Cathedral to offer his thanks to the Lord. Instead of the usual offering of battle trophies, he made an extraordinary gesture on at Wawel on April 8, 1794: he named three peasants, Bartosz Głowacki, Stanisław Świstacki, and Jędrzej Łakomski, standard bearers of the Grenadier Regiment. In this symbolic manner, Kościuszko made Wawel Cathedral the place where a great process of social change began.

Prince Józef Poniatowski also came to Wawel to take part in a great feast of thanksgiving celebrated on August 15, 1809, after the entry of the Polish army into the former national capital.

During the years of lost independence, Wawel Cathedral became the main shrine of the Polish p e o p l e. There were solemn commemorations of the anniversaries of great historical events, to which pilgrimages came from all three of the partitions into which Poland had been divided.

TREASURY
OF ART

Historians of art are fond of repeating that, from an architectural point of view, Wawel Cathedral is not a particularly successful building. This is true — except that, for all its drawbacks, this Cathedral is one of the most priceless landmarks of Polish art. Except that it has been a living masterpiece for centuries and centuries. Except that almost every generation has made its own contribution to the Cathedral's present shape.

This is why it is impossible to establish for certain that the Cracow Cathedral was designed by this or that architect, or that any one person built it. There is no way even to enumerate all the architects and builders who laboured at its erection, beautification, remodelling, or restoration. It includes the work of such masters as Veit Stoss, Bartolomeo Berrecci, Giovanni Maria Padovano, Jan Michałowicz of Urzędów, Giovanni Trevano, and Francesco Placidi. Above all, however, it is the work of artists — foreign and domestic — who are for the most part anonymous: architects and painters, sculptors, goldsmiths, and so on. This is also why the criterion of purity of style, so important in the evaluation of most buildings, cannot be applied. Because it has served for seven centuries in the role of the principal shrine of the state and the people, we must regard Wawel Cathedral as a building that has in fact never been finished, that has always been in the process of remodelling or renovation when it has not actually been under construction. Once we have accepted this primary assumption, it is easier for us to appreciate its unique charm and particular beauty.

The walls of the Tower of the Silver Bells and the attractive Crypt of St. Leonard date back to the period when Władysław Herman ruled. The crypt originated in the late eleventh or early twelfth century. Thanks to the skill of Adolf Szyszko-Bohusz, who served the Cathedral so well, we can enjoy the beauty of this finest example of Polish Romanesque architecture today. It consists of three naves divided by eight columns arranged in rows of four, supporting the cross-vaulting of the crypt.

In its main outline, the Cathedral is a three-nave Gothic construction with
a transept and an apse that surrounds the presbytery. Around it stand nineteen
chapels (counting the sacristy, which was formerly the Chapel of St. Margaret).
These chapels were originally Gothic in style. Over the years, some were
pulled down to make way for new ones, but many were remodelled. The Holy
Cross Chapel, which contains several priceless monuments — the two triptychs
on the altar, the splendid sarcophagus of Casimir the Jagiellon carved
by Veit Stoss, and of course the eastern frescoes — has retained its original
Gothic character. The Gothic construction of the Holy Trinity Chapel has
also been preserved, although its decoration has nothing in common with the
Middle Ages. The Gothic period is recalled above all by three royal sarcophagi:
those of Władysław Łokietek, Casimir the Great, and Władysław Jagiełło.
The Miraculous Crucifix of Wawel, placed form the start on the altar
at the entrance to the sacristy, also dates from the second half of the
fourteenth century.

The Renaissance left a distinct mark on the history of the Cathedral. Most
of the Gothic chapels were rebuilt in the sixteenth century. Each of them contains
works of the highest calibre: memorials, statues, altars. The unquestioned
pearl is the famous Sigismund Chapel with its lovely interior design, its masterpiece
of a silver altar, and the three delightful tombs of Sigismund I the Old,
Sigismund Augustus, and Anna Jagiellonka. The Cathedral contains innumerable
treasures of Renaissance art: the stone niche with the tomb of John
Albert in the Chapel of Bishop Jan Grot, the tomb of King Stefan Batory
in the Chapel of the Blessed Virgin, and the tombs of bishops Filip Padniewski, Piotr
Gamrat, Piotr Tomicki, Samuel Maciejowski, and others. The glories of the
seventeenth century are capped by the high altar, the Confession of St. Stanislaus,
the coffins of the martyrs and the Vasa Chapel.

The later classical epoch also beautified the Cathedral to a significant degree.
In the mid-nineteenth century the beautiful Potocki Chapel was rebuilt in the spirit of
late classicism. The Cathedral itself acquired, among other things, sculptures

by the famous Danish artist Bertel Thorvaldsen. This survey, brief as it may be, gives us an idea of the value of the architectonic and sculptural values of the decoration of the Cathedral. It would be unthinkable now to pass over the Cathedral treasury.

The building of the treasury, entered through the sacristy, was built at the end of the fifteenth century by Hanusz Blatfuss of Košice. The items found in the treasury today represent only a small percentage of what has been deposited here over more than a thousand years. By the beginning of the twelfth century the inventory of the treasury already included more than 300 objects, including gold and silver chalices, crosses, candelabras, reliquaries, chasubles, and copes. The treasury inventory from 1563 that is preserved in the Cathedral archives amounts to 180 pages of folio manuscript. It tells us, among other things, that the treasury then contained about 120 chalices, 170 monstrances, crosses, and reliquaries, 150 candlesticks, and 600 decorative chasubles and copes.

Many of these treasures were lost to war and looting. Nevertheless, there are still objects of the highest value left in the treasury today. These include the spear of St. Maurice, which was presented to Bolesław the Brave by the German emperor Otto III in 1000 A.D. There is a cross with the diadems of the Blessed Kinga and Bolesław the Bashful. There are the ring, paten, and chalice recovered from the grave of Bishop Maurus, who died in 1118. Among many priceless boxes, one, which Jadwiga is said by legend to have brought with her on her wedding journey in 1384, stands out. There are bishops' crosses and croziers. There are priceless reliquaries, including boxes for the head of St. Florian (the gift of Queen Zofia) and of St. Stanislaus (the gift of Elżbieta Rakuszanka). There are many monstrances with amazing designs. Objects related to great rulers and important historical events are also preserved in the treasury. In 1882, an inlaid pin recovered from the supposed grave of Bolesław the Bold in Ossiach was deposited here. There is also the sword of Sigismund the Old, broken during the funeral of Sigismund Augustus , the last king of the Jagiellonian dynasty. There is the stirrup of Kara Mustafa, the Turkish commander at the Battle of Vienna, sent by King John III Sobieski to his wife immediately after the battle with a sheet of parchment attached bearing the message 'He, whose foot was in this stirrup, has by the grace of God been conquered'. Nor is there any shortage in the treasury of chasubles and copes. These include a chasuble embroidered with pearls and donated in 1504 by Piotr Kmita. There are the coronation robes of Michał Korybut and Stanisław August Poniatowski.

The Cathedral library also deserves mention. It was founded in the eleventh century. By 1110 it already included 53 books. Over the years, the collection grew. Despite wars and looting it contains today 230 priceless illuminated manuscripts, 170 incunabula, and approximately 500 antiquarian books. There is a manuscript of 'Predicationes' from the late eighth century. There is a 'Pontificale' dating from approximately 1100 and decorated with plant and animal initials. There is the priceless 'Emmeram Gospel' made by the Benedictines in Regensburg and brought to Cracow about the year 1100 by Władysław Herman's wife Judith. Thirteenth-century manuscripts that are themselves copies of even earlier works make up another part of the library's invaluable collection.

There is only one way to conclude this review: those who say that the Wawel Cathedral is a true treasure house of art are right. The building itself depicts the shifts in artistic taste among our ancestors. In itself, it is a guidebook to the history of Polish culture. Its interiors contain a wealth of accomplishments by domestic masters, and by craftsmen and artists from East, West and the South. No other sacred building in Poland, or perhaps in Europe, testifies so unequivocally to the truth that in the world of art, there are no borders. Nor does any other building offer such visible proof of the simple fact that art does not divide, but unites people and nations.

IN THE SPLENDOUR
OF LEGEND

For centuries Wawel Cathedral had mighty protectors: generous monarchs, valiant commanders, devout bishops, and learned canons, not to mention the great lords anxious to inscribe their names in its history. With the fall of Poland at the end of the eighteenth century, however, most of these protectors disappeared. Now there were no more Polish kings or courageous commanders, and the great lords had turned their attention elsewhere. Even the true ruler of the Cathedral, the bishop, was gone. After all, for 44 years, as mentioned above, the Cracow Diocese was governed by administrators. In the meantime, it turned out that in these years of abandonment, and even of doubts about the future, the great legend of Wawel Cathedral was born. This is confirmed by the researcher, Stanisław Windakiewicz. In his history of Wawel, he writes, 'The many poetic works about Wawel from the first half of the nineteenth century show that Polish poetry finally took over guardianship of Wawel'.

Stanisław Wyspiański took up the theme many times. A particular place in his work belongs to the most beautiful 'song of Wawel' yet created in Polish poetry: the play 'Akropolis'. The Cathedral is more than a 'stone chronicle' of the past in this work: it becomes a source of life. 'Akropolis' is above all an epic of hope in the future resurrection of the nation.

The legend of the Wawel shrine includes many themes and motifs. It was created by artists of the stature of Wyspiański, but it is filled out most often by poets of lesser genius. There is a significant division of roles in the construction of the legend. Wyspiański, Pol, Ujejski, and Wasilewski were interested above all by what they found in the naves and the crypts, while authors of a lower order, and the anonymous ones, regarded the Cathedral from two different points of view: from above (the towers, the Sigismund Bell) or from below (the cellars).

It is worth looking at just these two latter aspects of the legend, above all because they have the widest scope. They have entered the folk legends about

the Cathedral. They also show how deeply the Cathedral is embedded in the collective Polish consciousness.

Ten bells hang in the towers of Wawel Cathedral. The oldest, the 'Nowak', was cast in the thirteenth century. Two bells, the 'Cardinal' and the 'Urban', were donated to the Cathedral in the mid-fifteenth century by Cardinal Zbigniew Oleśnicki. There are also the 'Goworek', the 'Maciek', and the 'Half-Sigismund', as well as two clock bells and one plaque bell. Only one bell, the 'Sigismund', has become extraordinarily famous. It was cast on the orders of King Sigismund I the Old in 1521 from cannons captured at the battles from the Walachians. It has a diameter of 2.5 metres, a circumference of 8 metres, and is two metres high. It was hung in the tower on July 9, 1521. It is significant that the unusually beautiful tone of this bell has spawned folk legends with a life of their own. Thus, it is repeated in Cracow that the bell owes the colour of its tone to many people. Some are convinced that the secret lay with a famous lutist and composer from Transylvania who, during the casting process, threw the strings of his lute into the vat of molten metal. Others say that the 'Sigismund' owes its sound to the wedding ring of the bell-maker's mother. Still others state that King Sigismund threw his sceptre into the casting vat, or that it was the mace of one of the military commanders, or a sword notched in battle, or that it was a bishop's crozier, or the hammer of an otherwise unremembered craftsman, a farmer's ploughshare, or the medal of a mother who had lost two sons fighting for Poland. Wherever the truth may lie, one thing is certain: the inhabitants of Cracow believe that the sound of the Sigismund Bell drives away the clouds and brings good weather. And that girls who touch its clapper will unfailingly find husbands and be happy in love.

A beautiful legend about the cellars of the Cathedral is equally widespread. The folklore of many European nations includes tales of great warriors and monarchs sleeping in inaccessible grottoes and caves, waiting for the signal that will bring them back to life and renewed deeds of valour. Polish folklore includes various reports of the knights of Bolesław the Brave or Bolesław the Bold sleeping in the grottoes of Giewont, or of the knights of St. Jadwiga of Silesia awaiting reawakening in the cellars of the Church in Trzebnica. These folk legends have also been connected with Wawel Cathedral. Since the mid-nineteenth century they have appeared time after time in various collections of fairy tales and legends, and also in literary works. We can thus read of a great chamber carved in the cellars of the Wawel Cathedral, where all the rulers of Poland lie waiting for the signal to set out to battle for a free Poland.

No one can say how much truth there is in any of this. No one can say whether Bolesław the Brave and Stefan Batory in fact led the Polish armies in their fight for the homeland during the First World War. Poets in any case were convinced that here and there Polish kings were seen dressed in the grey uniforms of Piłsudski's Legions, accompanying the soldiers in their marches and battles. One thing is sure: Wawel Cathedral together with its religious and national treasures, with its graves of kings and heroes in their eternal sleep, makes up an integral part of the great national legend of Poland. It has every right to this position: as Poland's most valuable jewel, as a building in which 'everything is Poland', as a stone chronicle of Church and country, as the Polish Zion, as a treasury of art and the altar of the fatherland, the seat of great bishops and the temple of the Polish kings. As a Cathedral that belongs to every Pole.

This album is also published in Polish, Italian, French, and German.

The photographs in this album were taken on Fuji and Agfa film and developed in the Foto-expert laboratory, 13 Karmelicka St., Cracow.

Engravings on pages 171–201 from the collections of the Jagiellonian Library and the State Art Collection at Wawel.

Wydawnictwo Postscriptum, Kraków 1993
31-026 Kraków, ul. Radziwiłłowska 29
First edition
Typesetting „Edycja", 1 Długa St., Cracow

Coordination: Paul Gerin
Warszawa tel./fax: (48-22) 27 96 20
Printed in Austria by Paul Gerin